MAKING MUSIC

MAKING MUSIC

TEXT AND PHOTOS BY
ARTHUR K. PAXTON

CONCEPT BY HELEN SIVE PAXTON

ATHENEUM NEW YORK 1986

ACKNOWLEDGEMENTS

Very special thanks go to David Amram, whose unique talents as composer, conductor, and communicator helped inspire this book.

Also thanks to Ken Adams, David Frost, Marion Guest, Karen Lindquist, Danny Seidenberg, Sandra Walker, and the other musicians of the Brooklyn Philharmonic Symphony Orchestra; and to Ben Altman, the Amram Family, Robin Bromley, Maurice Edwards, Ross French, Corodon Fuller, David Graham, Emily Granrud, John and Joshua Howe, Mike Jonnes, Barna Ostertag, Daria Paxton, Robert Paxton, Philip and Nathaniel Stern and Jack Sullivan.

Library of Congress Cataloging-in-Publication Data

Paxton, Arthur K.   Making Music

SUMMARY: Text and photographs follow a composer as he writes a piece of music, rehearses it with an orchestra, and has it played at a concert.
1. Music appreciation — Juvenile literature.
[1. Music] I. Paxton, Helen. II. Title.
MT6. P3F7 1986   780'.1'5   85-21471
ISBN 0-689-31119-2

Published simultaneously in Canada by
Collier Macmillan Canada, Inc.
Composition by Boro Typographers, New York City
Printed and bound by Maple-Vail, Binghamton, New York
Designed by Suzanne Haldane
First Edition

to Dorothy Paxton

MAKING MUSIC

Davids is a composer — he makes music.
One day he just sat and imagined new sounds.

4

He tried to make them at the
piano.

He played one note...

high notes...

quiet notes...

6

many notes...

low notes...

loud notes.

But David kept thinking of other sounds.

The sounds of musicians who

blew...   plucked...

bowed...   and struck.

12

If David conducted and they all played together,
what a glorious sound they would make!
And David knew just when they could do it.
He was going to conduct a series of concerts.

He would write a new piece for
orchestra. The new piece could
be played at the concerts along
with music by other composers.
    David got some music paper
and started to write down
his music.

Sometimes he went to the piano to work out his ideas and to check what he had written, but he always imagined the sound of an orchestra.

When he finished writing his piece, a copyist wrote out the parts for all the players.

The players got their parts and practiced by themselves.

In the meantime people found out about the concerts from
announcements in the newspaper and on the radio.

The musicians needed to practice together, so one by one
they showed up at the rehearsal hall

and got out their instruments.

They all tuned up — even the tympanist.

Then everyone began to play.

David used his baton to show the beat and to keep the
musicians together when the music went faster or slower.

He used his left hand to give cues and to show the musicians
whether to make the music sound sweet or angry or joyful.

And when people played too loud he let them know!

After several rehearsals everyone played together
beautifully. The only thing missing was the kind of
excitement that comes from playing for a live audience.

Some people came early to the first concert just as the orchestra was starting to go out onto the stage.

The oboist played an "A" and the orchestra tuned up.

When David gave the downbeat,

music filled the hall.

The concerts featured a variety of pieces in different styles
and moods.

One piece started with cellos and double basses

and got very loud when the trombones and tuba came
roaring in.

A flute player then switched to a piccolo and was
easily heard over the whole orchestra.

Each concert ended with
David's new music.
The audience

listened

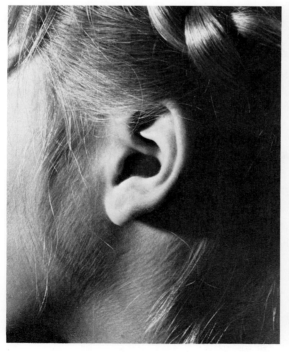

and listened

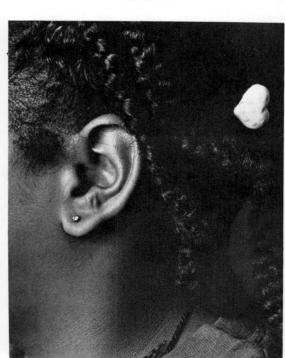

and listened

and listened

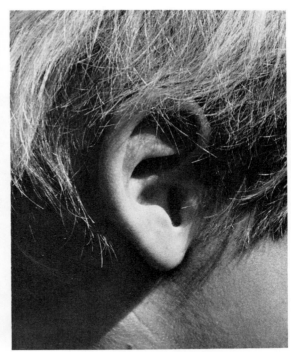

and listened

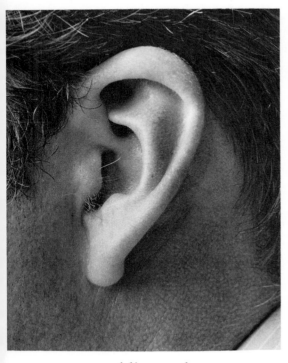

and listened

and . . .

even helped conduct!

Violinists made their instruments sing.

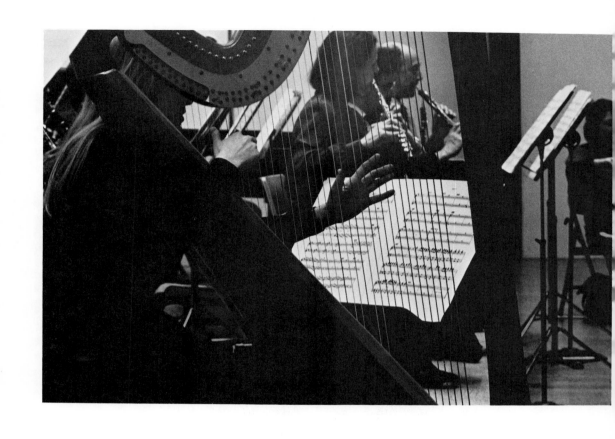

A harpist plucked dance rhythms,

and the brass and woodwinds played rich-sounding chords.

The piece ended with booming strokes on the tympani.

The audience clapped and shouted, "Bravo!" Some people
stood up. David beamed as he waved for his players to
stand and share the applause.

Today it's raining outside, and David is alone with his flute.

The rain sounds like drums ... then like clapping ... and
David remembers his concerts

and the joy of conducting his own music.